Summer Blast
Getting Ready for Fifth Grade

Reading   Writing

Math

Art

Puzzles   and more!

Author
Wendy Conklin, M.A.

SHELL EDUCATION

Standards

To learn important shifts in today's standards, see the Parent Handbook on pages 123–128. For information on how this resource meets national and other state standards, scan the QR code or visit our website at http://www.shelleducation.com and following the on-screen directions.

Publishing Credits

Corinne Burton, M.A.Ed., *President*; Emily R. Smith, M.A.Ed., *Content Director*; Jennifer Wilson, *Senior Editor*; Robin Erickson, *Multimedia Designer*; Valerie Morales, *Assistant Editor*; Stephanie Bernard, *Assistant Editor*; Amber Goff, *Editorial Assistant*; Mindy Duits, *Cover Concept*

Image Credits

pp. 5, 6, and 12 iStock; All other images Shutterstock

Standards

Shell Education

5301 Oceanus Drive
Huntington Beach, CA 92649-1030
http://www.shelleducation.com
ISBN 978-1-4258-1555-4
© 2016 Shell Educational Publishing, Inc.

Table of Contents

Welcome to Summer Blast!

Dear Family,

Welcome to *Summer Blast: Getting Ready for Fifth Grade*. Fifth grade will be an exciting and challenging year for your child. There will be plenty of new learning opportunities, including more complex books to read and more work with fractions and decimals! Interesting new topics in science and social studies will help keep your child engaged in the lessons at school.

Summer Blast was designed to help solidify the concepts your child learned in fourth grade and to help your child prepare for the year ahead. The activities are based on today's standards and provide practice with essential skills for the upcoming grade level. Keeping reading, writing, and mathematics skills sharp while your child is on break from school will help his or her fifth-grade year get off to a great start. This book will help you BLAST through summer learning loss!

Keep these tips in mind as you work with your child this summer:

◆ Set aside a specific time each day to work on the activities.

◆ Have your child complete one or two pages each time he or she works, rather than an entire week's worth of activity pages at one time.

◆ Keep all practice sessions with your child positive and constructive. If the mood becomes tense or you and your child get frustrated, set the book aside and find another time to practice.

◆ Help your child with instructions, if necessary. If your child is having difficulty understanding what to do, work through some of the problems together.

◆ Encourage your child to do his or her best work and compliment the effort that goes into learning.

Enjoy spending time with your child during his or her vacation from school, and be sure to help him or her prepare for the next school year. Fifth grade will be here before you know it!

What Does Your Rising Fifth Grader Need to Know?

1. Identify morals and themes in various types of texts.

2. Identify and describe conflict, climax, resolution, and character development in stories.

3. Understand parts of words, including root words, prefixes, and suffixes.

4. Add and subtract fractions and decimals to hundredths.

5. Divide large numbers by multi-digit numbers using long division.

6. Understand coordinate planes and ordered pairs.

7. Know about bacteria and other major domains of life.

8. Understand solids, liquids, and other states of matter.

9. Know about the history of the United States, including the 13 colonies, the American Revolution, and the Civil War.

10. Learn about the states in the United States and their capitals.

Things to Do as a Family

General Skills

◆ Make sure your child gets plenty of sleep. Children this age need 9–11 hours of sleep each night. Even in the summer, establish bedtime routines that involve relaxing activities, such as taking a warm shower or reading.

◆ Help your child become organized and responsible. Have places for your child to keep important things. Take time to set up a schedule together. Use a timer to keep track of time spent on different activities.

Reading Skills

◆ Set a reading time for the entire family at least every other day. You can read aloud or read silently. Help your child choose books that are at comfortable reading levels and interesting to him or her.

◆ After reading, be sure to talk to your child about what they've read. Ask questions about the characters, the plot, and the setting. Encourage your child to share details from the books.

Writing Skills

◆ Encourage your child to write emails, texts, or letters to friends and family members who live near and far.

◆ Have your child create an online blog or keep a diary/journal about activities he or she is doing during time off from school.

Mathematics Skills

◆ Have your child estimate measurements while out in the community. For example: *This menu is about 8 inches wide. About how wide do you think the table is?*

◆ Involve your child in cooking dinner. This is a great way to teach about fractions as well as liquid and dry units of measure.

Summer Reading Log

Directions: Keep track of your child's summer reading here!

Date	Title	Number of Pages

Top 5 Family Field Trips

A Trip to a Zoo

Bring a blank world map on a clipboard with you. As you visit each animal, have your child read the information placard and determine the original location of the animal or species. Then, help him or her locate that country on the world map and color it in. You'll all be amazed by how diverse the animals in your local zoo really are!

A Trip to a Museum

Your first stop should be the gift shop. Have your child pick out five postcards of artifacts or paintings in the museum. Then, as you visit the museum, your child should be on the lookout for the five items he or she chose. It's an individual scavenger hunt! (Postcards usually have a bit of information about the pictured item to help you find it.) If he or she finds all five, you can celebrate the great accomplishment! Plus, your child gets to keep the postcards as memories of the day.

A Trip to a Library

Work with your child to find a paired fiction and nonfiction set to read. First, think of a topic your child likes to learn about. Your child can then use the digital catalog to search for books on that topic that match his or her reading level. He or she can choose one fiction book and one nonfiction book on the same topic, check them out, and enjoy expanding his or her mind!

A Trip to a Monument or Memorial

If you're able to visit a monument or memorial with your child, be sure to make it come alive for him or her. Ahead of time, look up some interesting stories about the person who is honored by the monument/memorial. Focus on stories about the person's childhood or early accomplishments, as those will be more relatable to your child. As you stand and look at the monument/memorial, tell the stories and ask your child to think about and describe what kind of monument/memorial could be built for him or her someday!

A Trip to a National Park

The National Park Service has a great program called Junior Rangers. Be sure you check in with the rangers at the visitors' center to see what tasks your child can complete to earn a Junior Ranger patch and/or certificate. Before you travel to the park, your child can also go to the WebRangers site (http://www.nps.gov/webrangers/) and check out your vacation spot, play games, and earn virtual rewards!

Top 5 Family Science Labs

Science Fun—Egg in a Bottle

http://scifun.chem.wisc.edu/homeexpts/EggInBottle.htm

Learn about air pressure using this easy experiment.

Science Fun—Dancing Raisins

http://scifun.chem.wisc.edu/homeexpts/dancingraisins.htm

Learn about carbonated beverages and carbon dioxide while having fun!

Science Fun—Candy Chromatography

http://scifun.chem.wisc.edu/homeexpts/candy.htm

Learn about the dye used in the common candies you enjoy.

Science Bob—Build a Fizz Inflator

http://sciencebob.com/build-a-fizz-inflator/

Learn about the reactions between acids and bases in this fun experiment.

Science Bob—How to Make Slime

http://sciencebob.com/make-some-starch-slime-today/

Learn about solids and liquids as you make your own substance.

Top 5 Family-Friendly Apps and Websites

Apps

Bonza National Geographic by MiniMega Pty Ltd

This app includes fun word games and puzzles using facts and images from National Geographic.

7 Little Words for Kids and 7 Little Words by Blue Ox Technologies

Use your knowledge of how words are built to solve these vocabulary word puzzles.

KenKen Classic by KenKen Puzzle

This clever twist on Sudoku requires kids to solve math problems and use logical thinking.

Websites

Figure This! Math Challenges for Families

http://figurethis.nctm.org/

The National Council of Teachers of Mathematics supports families through this site with math challenges that families can solve together.

Funbrain

http://www.funbrain.com/

Fun, arcade-style games covering a variety of concepts at all grade levels make this a great website for busy families.

Top 5 Games to Play in the Car

Which Do You Like More?

Ask questions of each other in which you have to analyze two similar nouns and decide which you like better and why. For example, one person may ask, "Do you like the sun or Earth more?" The other person picks one and explains why. (The elaboration of why is the most important part of this exercise since it practices a key difficult critical-thinking skill.) Make sure the child realizes that coming up with the comparisons is at times as important as choosing the answer. The two items in the question must be somewhat similar so that true analysis takes place.

Yes/No Critical-Thinking Questions

Many verbal games can be played with yes/no questions. Take any game that is traditionally a guessing game (Guess My Number) and make it a yes/no question game. You say, "I'm thinking of a number from 1 to 200." Children have to ask you yes/no questions with mathematically accurate vocabulary. They might say, "Is the number prime?" If a child asks a question without using mathematical vocabulary, don't answer the question. And definitely don't answer if anyone just takes guesses!

I Spy (with a Twist)

I Spy is a favorite car-ride game. However, it can get boring when you play with just colors, so add a small twist. Instead of always spying a colored object, spy objects that are certain shapes, distances, or textures. You might say, "I spy an oval." Or, "I spy something about a mile away." Or even, "I spy something bumpy." It certainly makes the game more interesting. And don't forget to allow yes/no critical-thinking questions. For example, "Is the object high in the sky?"

ABC Categories

Think of a category and name an object from that category for every letter of the alphabet. Make it more challenging by choosing more difficult categories or by having every person name an example for every letter. Popular categories are movies, characters from books, or things seen on vacation.

Favorites

Think of a topic, and then everyone names their favorite examples of that topic. Someone might say, "Movies." Everyone would name their favorite movies. Allowing different people to think of the category each time helps keep the game interesting for everyone. It's fascinating to children that everyone enjoys such different things.

Top 5 Books to Read Aloud

The Crossover by Kwame Alexander

The 2015 Newbery Award® Winner is written in verse, so it is just asking to be read aloud. The words flow as you find the rhythm in this fascinating book. The book tells the story of two brothers and their family. The boys are basketball stars, but they're also young men learning their way in the world. You and your child will enjoy this story of how a family grows and changes together.

Out of My Mind by Sharon M. Draper

Reading about this young girl with cerebral palsy will give your child a new perspective on the challenges he or she faces. Your child will be cheering the protagonist on as she discovers how to show her voice to those adults and children who can't see past her special need.

Number the Stars by Lois Lowry

Learn about the Holocaust through a young Danish girl's experience. This book will provide many opportunities to discuss this important historical time with your child. The story does not delve too deeply into the history of World War II, and there is not too much violence. It's a good way to introduce the topic to young readers.

When the Mountain Meets the Moon by Grace Lin

This book blends Chinese folk tales and mythology into a wonderful story. The story's themes include friendship, adventure, and hope. The book is a wonderful way to look back in history and learn about a culture that may be very different from your own.

Bud, Not Buddy by Christopher Paul Curtis

In this touching novel, Bud is searching for his father after the death of his mother. He begins the journey on his own, but he meets very interesting and engaging characters along the way. His earnest journey is an adventure you'll never forget.

#51555—Summer Blast

Week 1

This week, blast through summer learning loss by:

- ◆ using relative pronouns
- ◆ summarizing a story
- ◆ writing a story
- ◆ designing a T-shirt
- ◆ ordering numbers
- ◆ calculating area
- ◆ using estimation to solve problems
- ◆ using clues to learn about explorers
- ◆ multiplying with number cubes

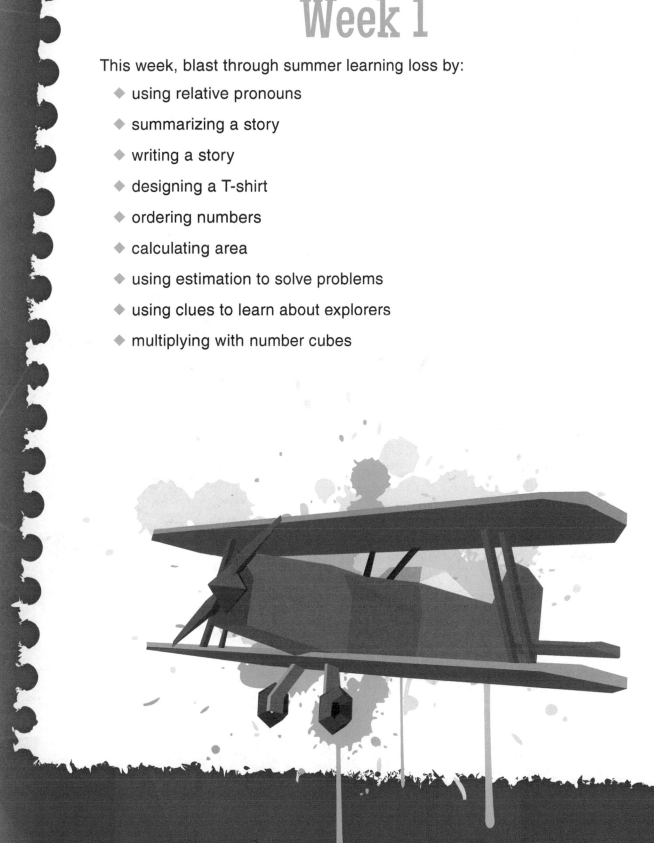

It's All Relative!

Directions: Complete each sentence with the correct relative pronoun.

A *pronoun* is a word that replaces a noun, such as *he*, *me*, or *we*.

A *relative pronoun* introduces a relative clause, which gives more information about a noun.

There are five relative pronouns: *that*, *which*, *who*, *whom*, and *whose*.

1. The letter _____ you gave me was very thoughtful and kind.

2. Babe Ruth, _____ is still considered one of the greatest athletes in all of American sports, will never be forgotten.

3. A fifth grader, _____ main job is to work hard in school, is still learning how to be responsible.

4. Ramona ordered the chocolate cake, _____ is why her sister made the same choice.

5. The library was full of students, almost all of _____ were looking for research books for their reports that are due on Friday.

6. My favorite pizza topping is pepperoni, _____ was the most popular response in the class survey.

USA 33

BABE RUTH

A Visit with Penguins

Directions: Read the passage. Then, answer the questions.

One of the penguins was ready to play. He waddled up the icy hill as fast as he could. Then, he flopped onto his stomach and slid down. Some of the penguins were eating lunch. They swallowed the fish as quickly as the zookeeper could empty the big buckets of food. A few of the penguins were sleeping quietly.

The children watched the penguins for a long time. When it was time to leave the exhibit, all the children were sad to go. Many of the children liked the penguin exhibit best.

1. Write one to two sentences to summarize the passage.

_____

_____

_____

_____

2. What do you think will happen next? Why?

_____

_____

_____

_____

Circus Balloon

Directions: Finish the story below. Include descriptive words in your story. Use the five senses (sight, sound, touch, taste, and smell) to add details.

A man from the circus filled the boy's large, red balloon with helium and tied it to a long ribbon. The boy held the ribbon tightly in his hand and walked over to see the enormous gray elephant. All of a sudden, a brisk wind . . .

_____

_____

_____

_____

_____

_____

_____

_____

_____

_____

_____

T-Shirt Designer

Directions: You are a famous T-shirt designer who designs for different charities. Use the template below to create your newest design!

Raffle Tickets

Directions: Place the raffle tickets in ascending order, and write the numbers below. Write each of the ticket numbers in standard form next to the number. The first one is done for you.

Number	Standard Form
1 6,942	six thousand, nine hundred forty-two
2	
3	
4	
5	
6	

Directions: Add 159 to each number below. Write the new number in digits and then in words. The first one has been done for you.

Number	+ 159	New Number
7 6,035	+ 159	6,194; six thousand, one hundred ninety-four
8 16,432	+ 159	
9 84,735	+ 159	

#51555—Summer Blast

Calculating Area

Directions: Calculate the area of each rectangle.

To calculate the area of a rectangle, multiply the length by the width.

❯ Area = length × width

❯ $A = l \cdot w$

18 ft.

7 ft.

$A = 18 \cdot 7$

$A = 126$ square feet (126 ft.²)

1

5 ft.

3 ft.

$A =$ _____

2

54 cm

43 cm

$A =$ _____

3

50 m

25 m

$A =$ _____

4

12 ft.

9 ft.

$A =$ _____

Solving by Estimating

Directions: Estimate to solve the problems.

Example

Jocelyn played 3 games on a social networking site. She received 321, 489, and 273 points.

About how many points did Jocelyn earn all together?

300 + 500 + 300 = 1,100 points

---

1 The same number of cats were curled up on each of 5 chairs. A total of 52 cats were curled up on these chairs. About how many cats were on each chair?

---

2 John caught 2,735 pounds of fish. He put them into boxes of 92 pounds each. About how many boxes did he need?

---

3 Ann played Math Martians on her computer. She scored 832 in the first game, 505 in the second game, and 397 in her last game. About how many points did she score all together?

Which Explorer Went Where?

Directions: Use the clues to find out why each explorer is famous. Use the chart to eliminate each one based on what you find out in the clues.

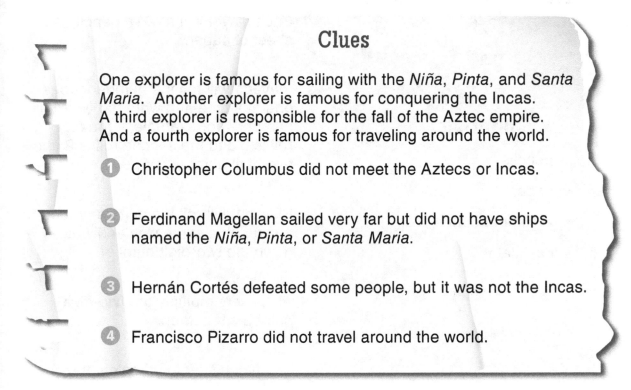

Clues

One explorer is famous for sailing with the *Niña*, *Pinta*, and *Santa Maria*. Another explorer is famous for conquering the Incas. A third explorer is responsible for the fall of the Aztec empire. And a fourth explorer is famous for traveling around the world.

1 Christopher Columbus did not meet the Aztecs or Incas.

2 Ferdinand Magellan sailed very far but did not have ships named the *Niña*, *Pinta*, or *Santa Maria*.

3 Hernán Cortés defeated some people, but it was not the Incas.

4 Francisco Pizarro did not travel around the world.

	Sailed *Niña*, *Pinta*, and *Santa Maria*	Conquered the Incas	Caused the fall of the Aztec Empire	The first to travel around the world
Francisco Pizarro				
Ferdinand Magellan				
Christopher Columbus				
Hernán Cortés				

Roll-the-Numbers Multiplication Game

Number of Players
2–6

Materials

◆ pencils

◆ paper

◆ 2 number cubes

◆ calculator

Directions

1 Each player will need a pencil and a sheet of paper.

2 Player 1 will roll the number cubes one at a time and write the two-digit number. For example, if the first roll is 6 and the second roll is 2, the two-digit number is 62.

3 Player 1 will roll the number cubes again in the same way and write down the two-digit number.

4 All players multiply the two-digit numbers together.

5 The first player to complete the math problem correctly wins the round. Use the calculator to check the answers.

6 Continue playing multiple rounds. Use tally marks to keep score on a sheet of paper. The first player to score 10 tally marks wins the game.

Week 2

This week, blast through summer learning loss by:

- capitalizing and punctuating
- analyzing a recipe
- writing a newspaper article
- creating a flyer to advertise a movie
- writing numbers in different forms
- analyzing data on a line plot
- solving multistep word problems
- completing a puzzle with expressions
- discussing hypothetical questions

Sentence Emergencies

Directions: These sentences need your help! Be a sentence doctor, and fix these sentences. Rewrite the sentences using correct capitalization and punctuation.

1 the students in mr garcias class were reading charlottes web

_____

_____

2 what a wonderful day it is

_____

_____

3 jordan come play with us in griffith park

_____

_____

4 watch out michelle

_____

_____

Reading a Shake Recipe

Directions: Read the recipe. Then, answer the questions.

Ingredients		Equipment
1 cup orange juice, chilled $\frac{1}{2}$ cup milk $\frac{1}{4}$ teaspoon vanilla	1 16-ounce can pitted apricot halves, chilled 1 banana ground nutmeg	measuring cups measuring spoons can opener blender drinking glasses

1 Measure the orange juice, milk, and vanilla into the blender. Add the apricots and their juice. Peel the banana. Break the banana into four pieces; add to the blender.

2 With help from an adult, put the lid on the blender and blend the mixture until it is smooth. Pour the mixture into glasses. Sprinkle the tops with a little nutmeg.

3 Serve cold and enjoy. Makes 4 servings.

To make your table look special, add a vase of flowers and tie pretty bows around some colorful paper napkins. Use rusts, greens, and browns in the fall. A winter table looks nice with reds and greens and pinecones with ivy or greens from trees. Soft colors and small bunny decorations work well in the spring. Red, white, and blue decorations make a perfect table for the 4th of July.

1 The "Shake Recipe" could also be called . . .

- (A) "How to Make Your Table Look Special."
- (B) "How to Use a Blender."
- (C) "A Tasty Treat for All Seasons."
- (D) "How to Throw a Summer Party."

2 The last paragraph was written mainly . . .

- (A) to show that the 4th of July is the best time to have a party.
- (B) to show that apricot-banana shakes should only be served on a table.
- (C) to show how to tie bows around paper napkins.
- (D) to give ideas about how to decorate for the holidays.

Read All About It!

Directions: Write a newspaper article about an event in your neighborhood. Look at a newspaper to find examples of writing for three different purposes: to inform, to entertain, and to persuade. Then, choose a topic and write one type of newspaper article. Make sure to tell about the *who*, *what*, *when*, *where*, *why*, and *how* of the event.

_____

_____

_____

_____

_____

_____

_____

_____

_____

_____

_____

_____

_____

_____

_____

#51555—Summer Blast

Hollywood Star

Directions: You are a famous actor who will be starring in an upcoming movie. Create a flyer that tells the world about this movie starring you!

Express This Number

Directions: Complete the chart.

Standard Form	Word Form	Expanded Form
1 34,262		
2 781,415		
3	fifty-one thousand, five hundred twenty-seven	
4	nine hundred twenty-three thousand, three hundred thirty-four	
5		20,000 + 3,000 + 400 + 60 + 9

Line Them Up: Making Line Plots

Directions: Use the data about lengths of erasers to make a line plot. Then, answer the questions.

A *line plot* shows data on a number line with various symbols to show frequency, such as an *x*. An *x* is marked each time the same measurement appears. A line plot makes it easy to see which measurements appear most or least often.

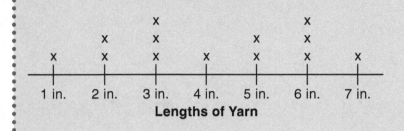

Lengths of Yarn

Lengths of Erasers

$3\frac{1}{2}$ inches //	$3\frac{1}{4}$ inches /
$2\frac{3}{4}$ inches //	$2\frac{1}{2}$ inches ///
$1\frac{3}{4}$ inches ///	$1\frac{1}{4}$ inches //
1 inch /	2 inches //

1 Plot the data on this line plot. Make sure to give the line plot a title and label the axis.

Title: _____

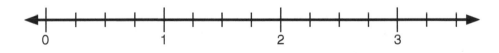

_____

2 What are the most common lengths of erasers? _____

3 What is the longest eraser? _____

4 What is the shortest eraser? _____

5 What is the difference between the longest and shortest erasers? _____

Multistep Word Problems

Directions: Solve the problems. Show the steps you take to find the answer.

1 Sergio enjoys collecting stamps as a hobby. He collected 12 stamps in June, 24 in July, and 29 in August. Then, he decided to give 18 to his brother. How many stamps does Sergio have left?

2 Lily ate 3 strawberries at breakfast and had 2 times that many for lunch. If she wants to eat 20 strawberries in one day, how many will she need to have for dessert?

3 Parker made 75 cents at his lemonade stand on Saturday. He made 2 times as much as that on Sunday. Parker wants to buy 2 candy bars that cost $1.00 each. Does he have enough money? If so, how much change will he get?

Many Ways to Say 10

Directions: Fill in the grid with the missing expressions.

Every mini-grid, every column, and every row must have each of these number sentences:

$$8 + 2, \ 10 \times 1, \ 20 \div 2, \ 15 - 5, \ 20 \times 0.5, \ 100 \div 10$$

	8 + 2	10 × 1			15 − 5
	20 × 0.5		8 + 2	10 × 1	
100 ÷ 10	15 − 5	20 × 0.5		8 + 2	
8 + 2	10 × 1		100 ÷ 10	15 − 5	
		15 − 5	10 × 1		8 + 2
10 × 1	20 ÷ 2				

Family Discussions

Number of Players

2–6

Materials

◆ *Discussion Cards* (page 103)

Directions

1 Cut apart the *Discussion Cards* on page 103, and place them facedown in a pile.

2 Each player takes a turn drawing a card and answers the question first.

3 In clockwise order, the other players take turns answering the question without repeating or copying what has already been said. Each player must support his or her answer with reasons why.

4 Once all players have commented on the card, discuss the similarities and differences between the responses.

5 Continue until all cards have been discussed.

If you could be any superhero, who would you be and why?

If you could be really good at something, what would it be and why?

If you could meet anyone, past or present, who would it be and what would you ask that person?

If you could be any animal, what would it be and why?

What do you believe is the most important job? Why?

If you could invent anything, what would it be and how would it help people?

Week 3

This week, blast through summer learning loss by:

- ◆ fixing run-on sentences
- ◆ analyzing opinions
- ◆ writing a narrative
- ◆ designing a dog park
- ◆ comparing numbers
- ◆ making equivalent fractions
- ◆ solving fraction word problems
- ◆ using clues to figure out a seating chart
- ◆ building a paper tower

Stop That Sentence!

Directions: Correct each run-on sentence by rewriting it into two sentences.

 **Tip** A sentence that combines two complete thoughts as one is called a *run-on sentence*.

1 My books are on the table my math book is on top.

_____

_____

2 They were closing the store it was time to go home.

_____

_____

3 Watch out for the slippery ice you could fall and hurt yourself.

_____

_____

4 I got a new blue shirt my blue shoes match perfectly.

_____

_____

5 My brother made the team will I be able to play baseball someday?

_____

_____

It's a Matter of Opinion

Directions: Read the opinion paragraph. Put a box around the opinion and underline the supporting details. Then, respond to the question.

Everybody needs to have a pet. Have you ever noticed that people who do not have pets are grouchier than those who do? If they were greeted whenever they came home by a furry creature thrilled to see them, they would be a lot less grouchy. A pet is affectionate and a good companion. Pets like to snuggle and be with people. Also, pets are always positive. If you give them a special treat, they act as if you've given them the world's largest diamond or the fastest car. They shake with joy, leap, and prance. If you've had a hard day, they still greet you with enthusiasm. They don't care what you do. You can be a complete failure, and they still treat you as if you were a king or queen. Pets love you unconditionally. If you forget to feed them, they forgive you the moment you remember. Pets are also good safety devices. They can scare away strangers. They can warn you if there is a fire or something wrong inside or outside the house. All they ask in return is a bowl of food, some water, and some TLC (tender, loving care). If everybody had a pet, everybody would go around smiling.

How does the author use reasons and evidence to support the opinion?

_____

_____

_____

_____

_____

_____

You're a Star!

Directions: Imagine that one day you become very famous. Write a story about the success that brings you fame. In the story, explain how and why you became famous. Also, tell about what other important things you might do in the future.

YOUR NAME

#51555—Summer Blast

The Most Outrageous Dog Park

Directions: You have been hand selected to create the most outrageous dog park. Draw an aerial view (view from above) of the park, and include a legend that explains each area.

Legend

Let's Compare!

Directions: Compare the numbers. Use the symbols >, <, or =.

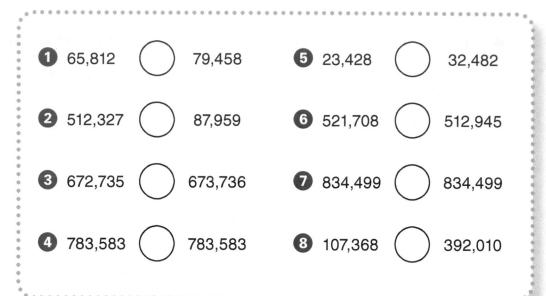

1. 65,812 ◯ 79,458

2. 512,327 ◯ 87,959

3. 672,735 ◯ 673,736

4. 783,583 ◯ 783,583

5. 23,428 ◯ 32,482

6. 521,708 ◯ 512,945

7. 834,499 ◯ 834,499

8. 107,368 ◯ 392,010

✏ **Choose a question, 1–8. Explain how you solved it.**

_____

_____

_____

_____

_____

Making Equivalent Fractions

To make equivalent fractions, multiply the numerator and denominator by the same number.

$$\frac{1 \times 2}{5 \times 2} = \frac{2}{10} \qquad \frac{1 \times 3}{5 \times 3} = \frac{3}{15}$$

Multiplying the numerator and denominator by the same number is the same as multiplying by 1.

Directions: Look at each fraction below. Write two more fractions that are equivalent in value.

1 $\frac{2}{3}$ = _____ = _____

2 $\frac{3}{8}$ = _____ = _____

3 $\frac{4}{5}$ = _____ = _____

4 $\frac{9}{10}$ = _____ = _____

5 $\frac{8}{13}$ = _____ = _____

Fraction Word Problems

Directions: Read the word problems. Show your work in the boxes.

1 Nola invited 15 friends to her birthday party. The girls ate pizza for dinner. They ate $\frac{2}{4}$ of the pepperoni pizza and $\frac{1}{4}$ of the cheese pizza. How much pizza did they eat altogether?

2 On Monday, Sergio made $\frac{3}{10}$ of his shots in the basketball game. On Tuesday, he made $\frac{1}{10}$ of his shots in the basketball game. What fractions of his shots did he make?

3 The cook needed to hard-boil some eggs. She used $\frac{1}{2}$ dozen eggs for breakfast and $\frac{3}{4}$ dozen eggs for lunch. How many eggs did she use altogether?

Dinner Table Seating Chart

Directions: Use the clues below to discover the seating chart for dinner.

Clues

George Washington, Benjamin Franklin, Thomas Jefferson, Alexander Hamilton, James Madison, and John Adams met for dinner. Benjamin Franklin chose the seat in the middle and next to the first president of the United States. The second president of the United States sat next to the third president of the United States. Thomas Jefferson sat across from George Washington. James Madison sat next to a person who never served as president. Alexander Hamilton sat across from the person who served as president during the War of 1812.

_____   _____   _____

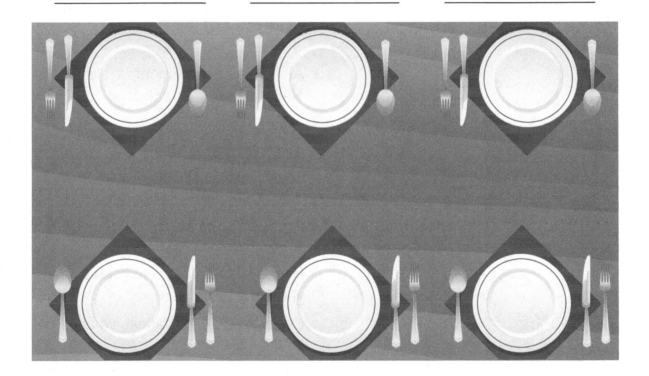

_____   _____   _____

The Tallest Paper Tower

Number of Players
2–6

Materials

◆ paper

◆ tape

◆ timer

◆ measuring tape

◆ scissors (*optional*)

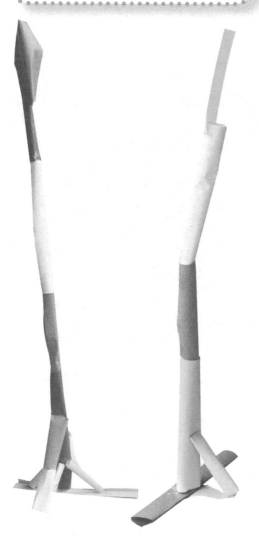

Directions

1 Distribute the same number of papers and one foot of tape to each player.

2 Each player will use the paper and tape to build the tallest tower in five minutes. Allow scissors to encourage cutting paper. **Note:** The tower must be able to stand on its own.

3 Allow two minutes for players to plan their towers.

4 Set the timer for five minutes and begin building the towers.

5 At the end of five minutes, players stop building.

6 Use the measuring tape to measure the paper towers. The person with the tallest paper tower wins!

7 Discuss the following questions:

◆ How could the tallest tower be improved upon?

◆ Besides being the tallest, what is the best thing about this tower?

◆ What are some other ways a person could build a taller tower?

Week 4

This week, blast through summer learning loss by:

- ◆ practicing homophones
- ◆ analyzing evidence to support claims
- ◆ writing a persuasive letter
- ◆ designing a room
- ◆ rounding decimals
- ◆ matching fractions to expressions
- ◆ solving fraction word problems
- ◆ solving a brain teaser
- ◆ racing to solve math problems

To, Too, or Two?

Directions: Write the correct homophone of *to*, *too*, or *two* on the lines.

1 I'm going _____ be in a dance recital tomorrow. I'll be wearing

my new tutu, which is a little _____ big. _____ of

my friends will dance, _____. I'm _____ excited

_____ sleep, but I have _____ go _____ bed.

2 The leaves were falling from the trees as I walked _____

school. It must be fall, which I call autumn, _____. I know

that there are _____ more weeks until Halloween. I can't

wait _____ go trick-or-treating! My friend Alexa is going

_____ walk with me, _____. We will remember

_____ say "Thank you!" after we get our candy. I hope that I

get at least _____ lollipops _____ eat!

An Author's Use of Evidence

Directions: Read the text. Put a box around the author's claims or main points. Then, underline all evidence that is included to support each claim. Finally, answer the questions on a separate sheet of paper.

Dear Restaurant Manager,

Though I have enjoyed your food in the past, I believe that the quality of your business has suffered recently and that certain issues demand your prompt attention. Recently, I was in your pizzeria and was extremely disappointed in the service that I received. I arrived with my family and was told it would be a 30-minute wait. Over an hour passed before we were seated, and no one apologized for this inconvenience.

Though our server took our order promptly, we waited over 20 minutes for drinks and appetizers to arrive. When the food arrived, the order was wrong! The server was quite rude when we asked for the items that we ordered.

We were very surprised to see that your customer service has suffered so horribly. There was no mention of taking things off our bill, no visit from you, not even a thank you. I like to support local businesses, but I can't spend money on restaurant experiences such as this one.

Please check into this matter immediately and do what you can to change your customers' experiences. We want to be loyal customers, but we need to see some sign of improvement first before we will visit your pizzeria for a future meal.

Sincerely,
Fred Gandley

1 Were all claims supported by credible evidence? Explain.

2 Do you think the restaurant manager will change his actions? Explain.

Letter to the Mayor

Directions: Write a letter to your mayor asking him or her to consider a new facility in your town, such as a skate park or an arcade. In the letter, be sure to support your request with reasons why the facility should be built.

_____

_____

_____

_____

_____

_____

_____

_____

_____

_____

_____

_____

_____

_____

Room Designer Extraordinaire!

Directions: You are an experienced designer and have been hired to create the most amazing room. In the sections below, either draw or cut out pictures from magazines to show what this space will look like.

Fabric

Paint Colors

Furniture

Something Unusual

Rounding Decimals

Directions: Round each decimal to the nearest whole number.

1 50.8

2 96.24

3 21.075

_____   _____   _____

Directions: Round each decimal to the nearest tenths place.

4 5.89

5 13.73

6 45.32

_____   _____   _____

Directions: Round each decimal to the nearest hundredths place.

7 3.908

8 851.431

9 0.634

_____   _____   _____

10 Why must you round to the nearest hundredth when dealing with money? Explain your thinking using complete sentences.

_____

_____

_____

Match the Fraction

Directions: Match the fractions to the correct expressions.

1 $\frac{5}{6}$

2 $\frac{9}{6}$

3 $\frac{18}{10}$

4 $\frac{4}{10}$

5 $\frac{9}{5}$

6 $\frac{12}{8}$

A $4 \times \frac{1}{10}$

B $2 \times \frac{6}{8}$

C $5 \times \frac{1}{6}$

D $3 \times \frac{3}{6}$

E $9 \times \frac{1}{5}$

F $6 \times \frac{3}{10}$

Real World Fractions

Directions: Read the word problems. Solve the problems by multiplying the whole numbers by fractions. Show your work.

1 Chloe has 12 pencils. If $\frac{3}{4}$ of them are broken, how many pencils are broken?

Work It Out	Answer

2 Mr. Garcia baked 24 cupcakes. He will bring $\frac{1}{3}$ of them to a party. How many cupcakes will he bring to the party?

Work It Out	Answer

3 The soccer players kicked 18 soccer balls to the goal. If $\frac{2}{3}$ of the balls made it in the goal, how many soccer balls did not make it in the goal?

Work It Out	Answer

Connect the Dots

Directions: Connect all the dots by drawing only three continuous straight lines.

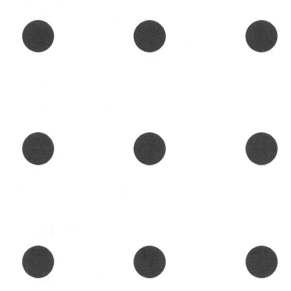

Reflection Questions

1 What was the first strategy you used to figure out this puzzle?

_____

_____

2 How many trials and errors did it take?

_____

_____

3 On a separate sheet of paper, create your own puzzle for someone to solve.

Who Can Solve It?

Number of Players
2–6

Materials

◆ *Math Problems Flashcards* (page 105)

◆ pencils

◆ paper

Directions

1 Each player will need a pencil and a sheet of paper.

2 Cut apart the *Math Problems Flashcards* on page 105, and place them facedown in a pile.

3 Each player takes a turn drawing a card from the pile and turning it over so that everyone can see it. The goal is to solve the problem on the flashcard as fast as possible.

4 The first person to complete the math problem correctly wins!

5 Repeat until all the cards have been solved.

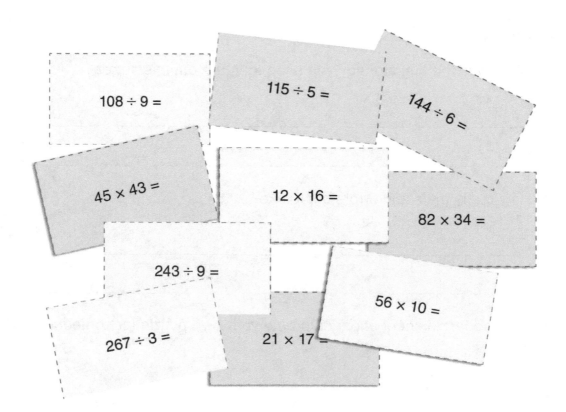

Week 5

This week, blast through summer learning loss by:

- using adjectives and adverbs in sentences
- making inferences
- researching and writing about domains of life
- creating an identity
- multiplying two-digit numbers
- turning fractions into decimals
- drawing and naming shapes
- identifying analogies
- making squares with toothpicks

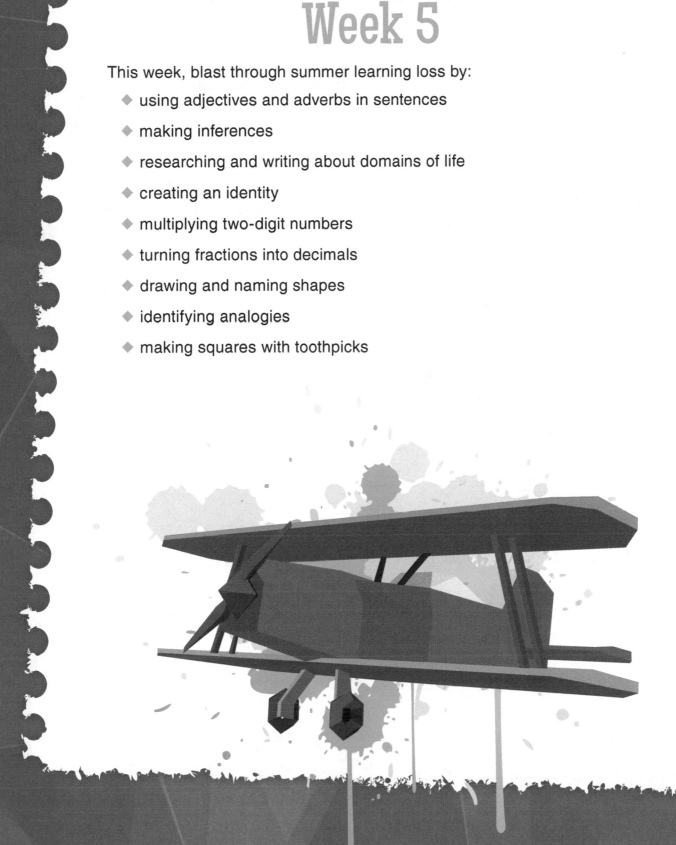

Adjectives and Adverbs

Directions: Add adjectives and adverbs to the sentences to make them more specific and interesting. Then, reread your sentences to make sure the adjectives are ordered correctly in each sentence.

Adjectives are used to modify nouns and pronouns. *Adverbs* are used to modify verbs, adjectives, and other adverbs. Both are used to make writing more specific and interesting.

Example without adjectives and adverbs: The convertible ran into the truck.

Example with adjectives and adverbs: The **red, shiny Mustang** convertible **suddenly** ran into the **four-door, white Dodge pickup** truck.

1 The dog barked at the cat.

_____

_____

2 I hit the ball.

_____

_____

3 Mei Ling ate lunch.

_____

_____

4 Everyone watched Rafael play basketball.

_____

_____

Inferring from a Picture

Directions: Look at the picture. Think about what might be happening. Then, answer the questions.

> Making an *inference* means to draw a conclusion based on given information. Some authors do not explain everything fully. They expect readers to "read between the lines."

1 What are the animals doing? How do you know?

_____

_____

_____

2 Why are the animals facing each other?

_____

_____

_____

It's Alive!

Directions: Research one of the three major domains of life (bacteria, archaea, and eukaryota). Use the Internet and/or nonfiction books to learn more about a domain. Write two paragraphs with facts and details about the domain.

True Identity

Directions: Below is a picture of a face. Who is this person—a villain, a princess, or someone else? Add to this face to reveal this person's identity.

Multiply Using a Standard Algorithm

Example: Multiply 67 × 43

Step 1: Multiply by the ones column.	**Step 2:** Multiply by the tens column. **Remember:** The 4 in the tens place represents 40.	**Step 3:** Add the partial products.
67 × 43 201 ← 3 × 67	67 × 43 201 2,680 ← 40 × 67	67 × 43 201 ← partial product + 2,680 ← partial product 2,881

Directions: Find the product using the standard algorithm.

1.　　46
　　× 32

2.　　51
　　× 69

3.　　25
　　× 84

4.　　94
　　× 16

5. Half of Mrs. Sullivan's 32 students brought in 12 notebooks each and the other half brought in 18 folders each. How many notebooks and folders do they have to share among all of the students?

_____

Turning a Fraction into a Decimal

A **decimal** is a fraction whose denominator is a power of ten (10, 100, 1000, and so on). The numerator in the fraction is written in the decimal place values to the right of the decimal point. A decimal, like a fraction, is not a whole number. It is part of a number.

$$\frac{4}{10} = 0.4 \quad \text{four tenths}$$

$$\frac{4}{100} = 0.04 \quad \text{four hundredths}$$

$$\frac{4}{1,000} = 0.004 \quad \text{four thousandths}$$

Directions: Change the fractions into decimals.

1 $\frac{5}{10}$ _____	2 $\frac{9}{10}$ _____
3 $\frac{2}{10}$ _____	4 $\frac{7}{100}$ _____
5 $\frac{4}{100}$ _____	6 $\frac{26}{100}$ _____
7 $\frac{80}{1,000}$ _____	8 $\frac{4}{10}$ _____
9 $\frac{6}{100}$ _____	10 $\frac{98}{100}$ _____

Features of Shapes

Directions: Draw and name each shape based on the description.

Description	Shape
1 • 3 sides • 1 right angle	
2 • parallel and perpendicular line segments • 4 right angles	
3 • 4 sides • acute and obtuse angles • 1 pair of parallel line segments	
4 • 4 sides • no right angles • 2 pairs of parallel line segments	
5 • 3 sides • only acute angles	
6 • parallel and perpendicular line segments • 4 right angles • all sides equal	

Awesome Analogies

Directions: Write a word to complete each analogy.

> **Example**
>
> teacher : student :: parent : child

1 pig : oink :: dog : _____

2 duck : quack :: cow : _____

3 fish : swim :: cheetah : _____

4 today : tomorrow :: yesterday : _____

5 gray : black :: pink : _____

Directions: Create your own analogies. Remember to include the colons.

6 _____

7 _____

Toothpicks and Squares

Number of Players
2–6

Materials

◆ *Direction Cards* (page 107)

◆ toothpicks

Directions

1 Each player begins by making this shape using 12 toothpicks.

2 Cut apart and shuffle the *Direction Cards* (page 107). Place the cards facedown in a pile.

3 Turn over a card to reveal the command.

4 The player who finishes the command first wins.

5 Set the toothpicks back to the shape above.

6 Then, repeat using a new card with a new command.

Week 6

This week, blast through summer learning loss by:

- ◆ sequencing sentences
- ◆ determining text structure
- ◆ writing a review of a movie or a television show
- ◆ creating art around a hole
- ◆ solving problems with remainders
- ◆ turning fractions into decimals
- ◆ multiplying whole numbers by fractions
- ◆ using clues to solve problems
- ◆ moving items in creative ways

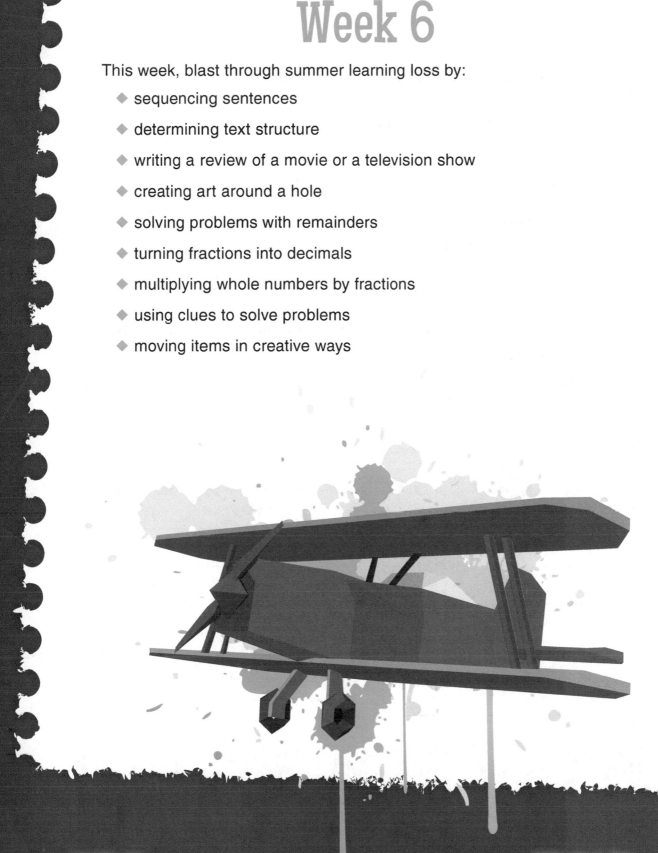

Put Them in Order

Directions: Read the sentences. Write numbers on the lines to place them in order. Then, write a paragraph to continue the story.

_____ I got out of bed and looked in the mirror.

_____ I ran to my mother to show her what had happened.

_____ She said, "It appears that those seeds you swallowed yesterday have been planted inside you."

_____ I woke up one morning feeling strange.

_____ Then, she looked in the phone book for a good gardener to come over to trim me.

_____ What a shock I got when I saw a plant growing out of my ears!

_____ I am feeling better now, but I still have to water myself every day.

_____

_____

_____

_____

_____

_____

_____

_____

_____

Identifying Text Structure

Directions: A text's *structure* is determined by the author's purpose for writing and the way he or she organizes the ideas. Use the chart to help you identify the text structure of the text below.

Text Structure	Definition	Signal Words
chronology	describes events or steps in order	before, first, next, soon, later, finally
comparison	shows how two or more ideas are alike and different	same as, similar, both, instead of, on the other hand
cause and effect	describes events and what made them happen	so, because, therefore, if, then, as a result, consequently, for this reason
problem and solution	describes a problem and possible solutions	question is, dilemma is, to solve this, one answer is, one option is

How to Make a Cabbage-Water Acid/Base Detector

First, take a head of red cabbage and cut it into strips approximately 1 cm (0.25 in.) by 4 cm (1.37 in.). Next, measure 50 grams (1.76 ounces) of the chopped cabbage into a glass beaker. Cover with 4 times the weight of the cabbage, which in this case will be 200 grams (7 ounces) of water. Heat the beakers at 800 degrees Celcius (1,472 degrees Fahrenheit) until the liquid begins to boil. Then, lower the temperature to 300 degrees Celcius (572 degrees Fahrenheit). Continue to cook the mixture for five more minutes. After five minutes, turn off the heat and allow the mixture to cool. Once it reaches room temperature, strain out the cabbage pieces and discard. The water should be bluish purple. It can now be used to determine whether substances are acids or bases. Acids will turn the water pink, while bases will react to turn the water teal.

Text structure: _____

Evidence: _____

_____

_____

Movie Review

Directions: Write a review of a movie or TV program. Include details about the plot and descriptions of the characters. Give specific details to support your main idea, and include how various techniques used by the actors and producers contributed to the message or main idea of the movie.

There's a Hole in My Paper!

Directions: What can you draw that has a hole in it? Draw a picture that incorporates this hole in a creative way.

What's Remaining?

Some division problems divide evenly, and other times, you are left with remainders.

$$27 \div 9 = 3$$

But what happens when you divide 29 by 9?

9 divides into 29 3 times, but there are 2 left over.

This solution has a remainder of 2. It can be written 3 R2.

Directions: Solve the problems. The answers may or may not have remainders.

1. $8\overline{)9}$

2. $9\overline{)39}$

3. $6\overline{)96}$

4. $4\overline{)87}$

5. $7\overline{)102}$

6. $3\overline{)22}$

7. $6\overline{)648}$

8. $8\overline{)113}$

9. $5\overline{)125}$

Getting Decimals in Line

Directions: Change each group of fractions into decimals. Then, place the decimals in order from greatest to least.

1 $\dfrac{5}{10}$ $\dfrac{9}{10}$ $\dfrac{6}{100}$ $\dfrac{7}{100}$

_____   _____   _____   _____

2 $\dfrac{9}{10}$ $\dfrac{6}{100}$ $\dfrac{4}{100}$ $\dfrac{61}{1,000}$

_____   _____   _____   _____

3 $\dfrac{4}{10}$ $\dfrac{12}{100}$ $\dfrac{8}{10}$ $\dfrac{2}{1,000}$

_____   _____   _____   _____

4 $\dfrac{9}{10}$ $\dfrac{6}{1,000}$ $\dfrac{9}{100}$ $\dfrac{57}{100}$

_____   _____   _____   _____

Directions: Mark the letter of each value in the correct location on the number line.

0   1

5 **A**   0.75

6 **B**   0.29

7 **C**   0.15

8 **D**   0.50

Fraction Party Riddles

Directions: Read the word problems. Solve the problems by multiplying the whole numbers by fractions. Show your work.

1 The Niles family is having a barbecue. They are inviting family and friends. If they want to grill $\frac{2}{3}$ pound of ribs for each person and 15 people are eating ribs, how many ribs do they need to grill?

2 Some people at the Niles family party will be eating salmon. If the Niles family wants to cook $\frac{3}{5}$ pound of salmon for each person and 12 people are eating salmon, how much salmon do they need to cook?

3 The Niles family wants everyone to eat dessert, too. If they estimate that each guest will have about $\frac{1}{6}$ of a pie, how many pies do they need to serve 24 guests?

What Happened?

Directions: Read the scenarios. Then, describe what happened.

Jack is inside a boot. Puddles of water and glass surround the boot on the floor. He won't survive unless he is submerged in water soon. In the space below, explain what you think happened.

_____

_____

_____

_____

_____

_____

You drive a limousine. There are six people inside, including three adults and three children. Two of them are female and the rest are male. Most of the passengers have either blue or green eyes, but one has brown eyes. What color are the driver's eyes?

_____

_____

_____

_____

_____

_____

Move Those Things!

Number of Players
2–6

Materials

- 3 marshmallows
- 1 egg
- 1 balloon (blown up)
- 1 tennis ball
- 1 tablespoon
- 3 toothpicks
- 3 pencils
- 6 paper clips
- timer

Directions

1 Place all the items on the counter.

2 Work as a team to move the items from the counter to a table at least four feet (1.2 meters) away.

3 Your teammates cannot touch the items with their hands. Instead, move the items using these utensils: tablespoon, toothpicks, pencils, and paper clips. These utensils can only be used one time.

4 Set the timer for five minutes, and see if your team can do this task!

5 When the time is up, talk about the activity using these questions:

- How else could the items have been moved without dropping them?

- What would you change if given another chance to move these items?

- What else would you add to these utensils to help you move the items more easily?

Week 7

This week, blast through summer learning loss by:

◆ using clues to figure out vocabulary

◆ learning about the Battle of Shiloh

◆ writing about a funny moment

◆ describing steps to draw a picture

◆ using long division to uncover a message

◆ calculating areas

◆ figuring out times

◆ learning about important Americans

◆ experimenting with dough and weight

Clue Me In!

Directions: Read about these natural elements. Use clues from the text to determine the meaning of each underlined word.

Aluminum

Aluminum is a natural element. Even though it is natural, it is never found on its own in nature. It has to be <u>extracted</u> from other minerals. It is used to make foil, cans, pots and pans, and even airplanes.

Clue: _____

Definition: _____

_____

_____

Iron

There is an <u>abundance</u> of iron in the universe. It is found inside Earth, in the soil, in water, and even in stars! Just about everywhere you look, this natural element can be found.

Clue: _____

Definition: _____

_____

_____

A Letter of Despair

Directions: Read the letter. Underline parts that include lots of description. Write notes in the margins about how the author has made you feel while reading the letter.

My Dearest Brother Frederick,

I have never imagined such horror as I have seen these last few days at Shiloh. There were so many men who left the mortal realm. There were so many women made widows. I am not sure I can bear to think upon it, but I know that if I do not write these things down, they will haunt me forever.

The first day of fighting was a clear Southern victory. General Johnston had learned Union reinforcements were on the way. He wanted to attack before they arrived. His plan was sound, but the fighting was fierce. I lived through the bloodiest day of the war thus far. May there never be another like it! General Johnston himself was slain by a cannon blast, and General Beauregard took over command. Our own dear friends, Kurt Flanders and Willem Simpson, fell. My heart grieves for them and for their families back home in Georgia.

General Buell arrived with Grant's reinforcements. Suddenly, the advantage was no longer ours. There were 45,000 men with the North. Our numbers were maybe half of that. In the end, General Beauregard was forced to withdraw our troops back to Corinth. The victory we had celebrated the day before felt like too little gain for too much loss.

Your Loving Brother,
John

That's Funny!

Directions: Write a journal entry about a funny or embarrassing moment in your life.

What Does It Look Like?

Directions: Draw one thing in the box below. Then, write detailed steps explaining how to draw it on the lines below. Have someone draw the same picture using your steps. Then, compare the pictures!

1 _____

_____

2 _____

_____

3 _____

_____

4 _____

_____

Get the Message!

Directions: Find the quotient using any method. Use scratch paper to help you. Match the solutions below to uncover a famous quotation by Abraham Lincoln.

T 15)567	**A** 4)600	**G** 6)1,425
W 12)879	**V** 60)903	**U** 3)852
J 36)5,490	**B** 5)6,214	**E** 25)625
H 18)600	**D** 82)7,545	**N** 10)3,045
O 19)361	**Y** 56)1,234	**R** 11)91

73 R 3	33 R 6	150	37 R 12	25	15 R 3	25	8 R 3

22 R 2	19	284

150	8 R 3	25

,

1,242 R 4	25

150

237 R 3	19	19	92 R 1

19	304 R 5	25

.

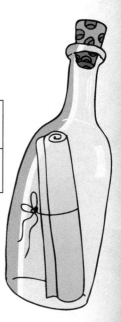

Accurate Areas

Directions: Measure each of these rectangles in centimeters. Round your measurements to the nearest centimeter. Then, calculate the area.

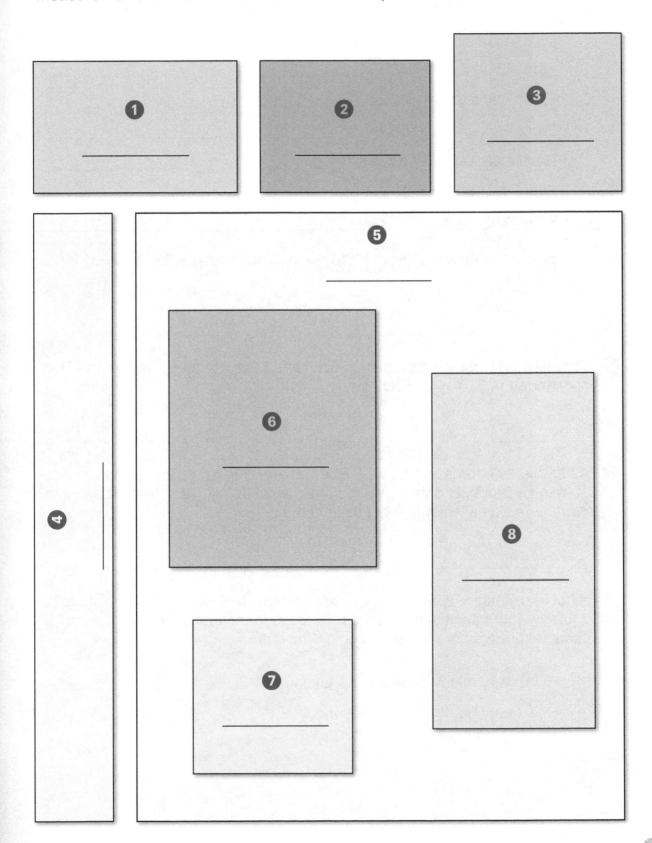

How Long Does It Take?

Directions: Read and solve each problems.

1 Calculate the length of time in hours and minutes between each of the following sets of times:

Ⓐ From 12:00 A.M. to 7:20 A.M. _____

Ⓑ From 7:20 P.M. to 11:10 P.M. _____

Ⓒ From 6:15 A.M. to 10:50 A.M. _____

Ⓓ From 2:05 A.M. to 3:10 A.M. _____

Ⓔ From 12:15 P.M. to 6:00 P.M. _____

Ⓕ From 7:10 A.M. to 11:25 A.M. _____

2 A movie at the theater starts at 7:10 P.M. and finishes at 9:25 P.M. How long does it run?

_____

3 Yi and Brian went to see a play, which lasted 2 hours and 12 minutes. The play ended at 3:04 P.M. What time did it start?

_____

4 A bicyclist left home at 6:30 A.M. She rode until 8:10 A.M., stopped for a 20-minute break, and then cycled home, which took 1 hour and 50 minutes. What time was it when she got back home?

_____

5 Nihal and Shanice drove from Chicago, Illinois, to Cincinnati, Ohio. It took 3 hours and 50 minutes to drive from Chicago to Indianapolis and 2 hours 25 minutes to drive from Indianapolis to Cincinnati.

Ⓐ How many minutes did the trip take in all? _____

Ⓑ How many hours and minutes did it take? _____

Who Is Responsible for What?

Directions: Use the clues to figure out who is responsible for what event in history. Match each person or persons with the correct event.

Clues

Teddy Roosevelt was a rugged man who loved hunting and the outdoors. Lewis and Clark lived for adventure and exploring new territories. Benjamin Franklin was constantly inventing things and making life easier for Americans. James Madison had a knack for writing laws. Martin Luther King Jr.'s famous speech was about his dream that his children would be treated the same as other children, regardless of skin color. A famous suffragist, Susan B. Anthony, gave speeches and had people sign petitions.

1 Who was responsible for helping to get women the right to vote?

_____

2 Who was responsible for going on an expedition west to discover new land?

_____

3 Who was responsible for working for equal rights for African Americans?

_____

4 Who was responsible for writing the United States Constitution?

_____

5 Who organized the first United States mail service?

_____

6 Who designated land to be protected by the United States National Park Service?

_____

Dough Boats

Number of Players
2–6

Materials

◆ clay or molding dough

◆ timer

◆ pennies or paper clips

Directions

1 Give each person the same amount of clay or molding dough.

2 Set the timer for 10 minutes. Players will use their clay or dough to create a boat that can hold the most pennies or paper clips.

3 Fill the sink with water, and place the boats in the sink. One by one, place a penny or a paper clip in each boat.

4 The last boat to stay afloat wins!

5 Discuss these questions after the contest.

◆ What was different about the boat that lasted the longest?

◆ Why do you think this boat stayed afloat with the most weight?

◆ What would you do to improve your boat?

Week 8

This week, blast through summer learning loss by:

- ◆ determining the meanings of idioms
- ◆ answering text-dependent questions
- ◆ writing step-by-step instructions for doing something
- ◆ drawing an amazing machine
- ◆ identifying patterns
- ◆ creating equations to reach a target number
- ◆ determining prices based on pounds
- ◆ thinking about genetics
- ◆ creating sentences from words

Idioms

Directions: Determine the meanings of the idioms.

 Tip *Idioms* are expressions with meanings different from the literal meanings.

1 When Angelica said, "That movie took my breath away," what did she mean?

_____

_____

2 "When Dad put his foot down, my brother did better in school," said Boris. What did Boris mean?

_____

_____

3 Dana stood and said, "I guess I'll hit the road now." What did Dana mean?

_____

_____

4 When Mario said that he was under the weather, what did he mean?

_____

_____

5 When Nicholas said that he slept like a log last night, what did he mean?

_____

_____

The Crazier the Better

Directions: Read the passage. Then, answer the questions. Use text from the story to support your answers.

To José, Crazy Hair Day was the best day of the school year. He loved being goofy, and he loved making his classmates laugh. On Crazy Hair Day, he usually managed to do both of those things very well.

In second grade, he colored his hair purple and spiked it into a cone shape like a troll doll. In third grade, he braided his hair into 16 tiny braids. He wrapped a pipe cleaner around each braid and stuck paper airplanes to the ends. He called his design Fly Boy. That was awesome!

This year would be no exception. José had been planning it since September. That's when he had found an abandoned bird's nest on the way to school. He had saved it in a plastic bag all these months. It was going to be the perfect Crazy Hair Day accessory!

1 Why does José like Crazy Hair Day?

_____

_____

_____

2 Describe José's third-grade Crazy Hair Day style.

_____

_____

_____

3 What do you think José plans to do for this year's Crazy Hair Day?

_____

_____

_____

Here's How You Do It!

Directions: Think of something you know how to do well, such as playing a sport or playing an instrument. Then, write step-by-step instructions that explain how to do it.

_____

_____

_____

_____

_____

_____

_____

_____

_____

_____

_____

_____

_____

_____

_____

_____

The Most Amazing Machine

Directions: You have invented the most amazing machine! Draw the machine. Then, add notes to the drawing to explain why it is the most amazing machine ever!

Looking for a Pattern Problems

Directions: Solve each problem and show your work.

Problem A

Complete each number line. Then, write the rule.

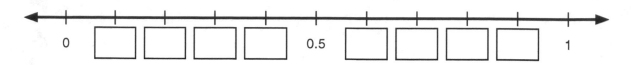

Rule: _____

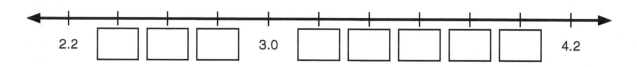

Rule: _____

Rule: _____

Problem B

Create your own number line. Then, write the rule.

Rule: _____

Target Number

Directions: Use the given numbers to reach each target number. You may use parentheses, multiplication, division, addition, and/or subtraction. Write your equation on the line provided.

---

1 Target number: 3

1	2	3	4	3

_____

---

2 Target number: 2

6	7	8	9	10

_____

---

3 Target number: 12

3	3	3	5	6

_____

---

4 Target number: 5

4	5	5	10	10

_____

Consumer Math

Directions: The Corner Market advertises their fruit prices by the pound on a chalkboard outside the store every week. Use the prices for this week to answer the questions.

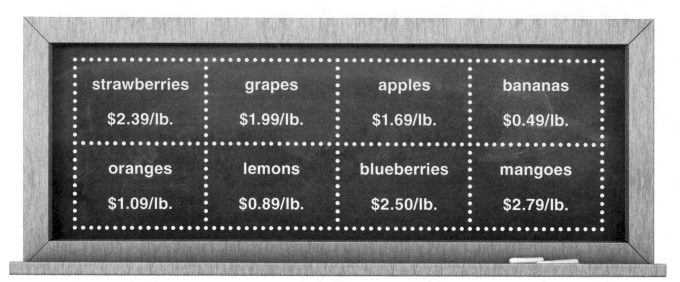

strawberries	grapes	apples	bananas
$2.39/lb.	$1.99/lb.	$1.69/lb.	$0.49/lb.
oranges	lemons	blueberries	mangoes
$1.09/lb.	$0.89/lb.	$2.50/lb.	$2.79/lb.

1 Charlie's grandmother gave him a $20.00 bill. If he buys 3 lbs. of bananas, 2 lbs. of oranges, and 3 lbs. of grapes, how much change will Charlie give back to his grandmother?

_____

2 Kathryn has 10 dollars and needs to buy 5 lbs. of strawberries. Will she be able to buy all 5 lbs.? Show how much over or under Kathryn will be.

_____

3 Hannah buys 1 lb. of each kind of fruit on the chalkboard. How much will this cost her?

_____

4 Mason is going to have a lemonade stand. His aunt buys him 10 lbs. of lemons. If he sells each cup of lemonade for a quarter, how many cups does he need to sell to pay her back?

_____

#51555—Summer Blast

How Does He Have Blue Eyes?

Directions: A wife and husband have a son with blue eyes. The wife has blue eyes. The husband has brown eyes. Blue eyes are recessive and brown eyes are dominant. Look over the information in the chart. Then, answer the question below.

Possibilities of Genotype

B = dominant brown

b = recessive blue

G = dominant green

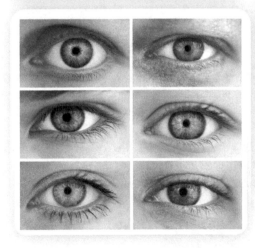

Genotype		Color of Eyes
BB	bb	brown
BB	Gb	brown
BB	GG	brown
Bb	bb	brown
Bb	Gb	brown
Bb	GG	brown
bb	GG	green
bb	Gb	green
bb	bb	blue

How it is possible for them to have a blue-eyed son?

_____

_____

_____

Word Sentences

Number of Players

2–6

Materials

◆ *Word Cards* (page 109)

◆ paper

◆ pencils or pens

Directions

1 Give each player a pencil or pen and a sheet of paper.

2 Cut apart the *Word Cards* on page 109, and place them facedown in a pile.

3 One player will turn over the top card.

4 Players will write four-word sentences using the four letters found in the words on the cards. (For example, **cats:** Can apples taste sour?)

5 The first player to finish each sentence gains a point.

6 Repeat until all cards have been used. The player with the most points at the end of the game wins.

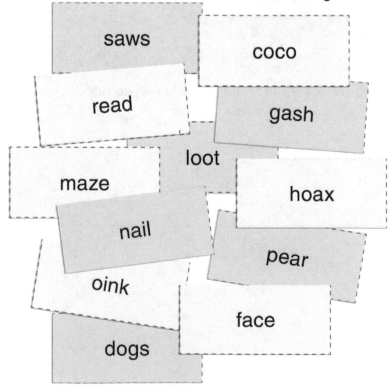

saws

coco

read

gash

loot

maze

hoax

nail

pear

oink

face

dogs

Week 9

This week, blast through summer learning loss by:

- ◆ ordering adjectives
- ◆ figuring out the theme of a poem
- ◆ writing from different points of view
- ◆ using thumbprints to create art
- ◆ using scientific notation
- ◆ classifying triangles
- ◆ solving multistep word problems
- ◆ identifying similarities and differences in geography
- ◆ putting words into categories

Order of Adjectives

Directions: Adjectives have a specific order when written in sentences. Use the Order of Adjectives Chart to help you write sentences.

Order of Adjectives Chart
opinion
size
age
shape
color
origin
material
purpose

1 Write a sentence using three adjectives to describe a family member.

_____

_____

_____

2 Write a sentence using three adjectives to describe your favorite food.

_____

_____

_____

3 Write a sentence using three adjectives to describe an animal.

_____

_____

_____

4 Write a sentence using three adjectives to describe a game.

_____

_____

_____

What Is the Theme?

A *theme* is the central idea of a literary work. It is a lesson, moral, or message about life. Sometimes, the author clearly states the theme. More often, the author implies the theme. The reader must use clues from the text to figure it out.

Directions: Read the poem. Then, answer the questions.

Block City
by Robert Louis Stevenson

What are you able to build with your blocks?
Castles and palaces, temples and docks.
Rain may keep raining, and others go roam,
But I can be happy and building at home.

Let the sofa be mountains, the carpet be sea,
There I'll establish a city for me:
A kirk and a mill and a palace beside,
And a harbor as well where my vessels may ride.

Great is the palace with pillar and wall,
A sort of a tower on top of it all,
And steps coming down in an orderly way
To where my toy vessels lie safe in the bay.

This one is sailing and that one is moored:
Hark to the song of the sailors on board!
And see on the steps of my palace, the kings
Coming and going with presents and things!

1 What is the theme of this poem?

_____

_____

2 What lines in the poem helped you figure out the theme?

_____

_____

My Family from Different View Points

Directions: Write a paragraph about your family from a third-person point of view. Then, write a revised paragraph that shows a different point of view.

_____

_____

_____

_____

_____

_____

_____

_____

_____

_____

_____

_____

_____

_____

_____

_____

_____

Thumbprint Pictures

Directions: Look at the thumbprints. What will these thumbprints become? Create a drawing around each one.

Solve That Notation: Unknown Quantities

Scientific notation is a shorter way to write numbers. To convert numbers to scientific notation, place a decimal point after the first number. The exponent indicates how many places the decimal will move. Move positive exponent decimals to the right.

$10,000 = 1 \times 10^4$	$53,000 = 5.3 \times 10^4$
$1,000 = 1 \times 10^3$	$5,300 = 5.3 \times 10^3$
$100 = 1 \times 10^2$	$530 = 5.3 \times 10^2$
$10 = 1 \times 10^1$	$53 = 5.3 \times 10^1$
0	0

Directions: Write each number in scientific notation.

1 40,000

2 75,000

3 3,000

_____

4 100,000

5 83

6 956

_____

Directions: Write each number in standard form.

7 6×10^3

8 8×10^4

9 3×10^2

_____

10 2.9×10^4

11 9.1×10^3

12 1.5×10^2

_____

Triangles

A *triangle* is a two-dimensional polygon with three sides and three angles. You can classify triangles in two different ways.

Classify by Sides

equilateral	isosceles	scalene
three equal sides; therefore, all sides are congruent	two equal sizes; therefore, two sides are congruent	no sides are equal; therefore, no sides are congruent
		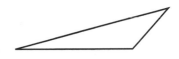

Classify by Angles

right	obtuse	acute
a triangle with one right angle, measuring 90°	a triangle with one obtuse angle, measuring greater than 90°	a triangle with only acute angles, each measuring less than 90°
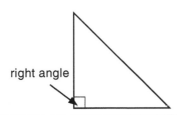	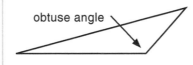	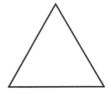

Directions: Classify each triangle by its sides and by its angles.

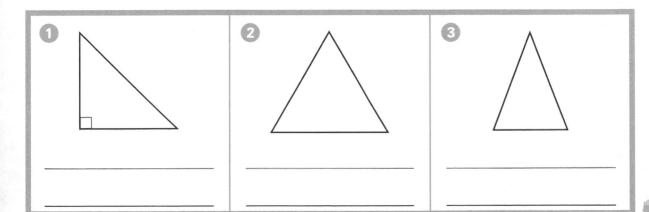

Solve That Word Problem!

Directions: Read the word problems. You will need to do more than one step to solve each problem. Show the steps you take to find each final answer.

1 Renee enjoys building model cars as a hobby. She built 13 cars in June, 18 in July, and 23 in August. Then, she decided to give 16 to her brother. How many cars does Renee have left?

2 Ann did 30 jumping jacks in the morning and did 3 times that many in the afternoon. If she wants to do 120 jumping jacks in one day, how many will she need to do at night?

3 Two large pizzas have 24 slices total. If 7 friends want to share the pizzas, and they each want 3 slices, is there enough pizza? If so, how much is left?

 #51555—Summer Blast

What Doesn't Belong?

Directions: Each problem contains one place that does not belong. Find the one that does not belong. Then, explain your answer on the lines.

1 North America, Brazil, Canada, New York City

_____

_____

2 Asia, Himalayas, Germany, Ganges River

_____

_____

3 India, Africa, Europe, Australia, Antarctica

_____

_____

4 Indian Ocean, Andes Mountains, Gulf of Mexico, Mediterranean Sea, Red Sea

_____

_____

5 Tokyo, Los Angeles, Mexico, Vancouver

_____

_____

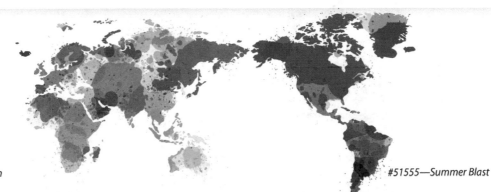

Categories

Number of Players

2–6

Materials

◆ *Category Cards* (page 111)

◆ *Letter Cards* (page 113)

◆ paper

◆ pens or pencils

◆ one-minute timer

Directions

1. Cut apart the *Category Cards* on page 111. Distribute one to each player or every two players.

2. Cut apart the *Letter Cards* on page 113. Shuffle and place them facedown in a pile.

3. Turn over a Letter Card. This card contains the letter you will use to begin a word for each category listed on the *Category Cards*.

4. Players will have one minute to come up with a word that begins with that letter for each category.

5. The first player to have a word for every category keeps that letter card.

6. Repeat until all cards have been used. The player with the most *Letter Cards* wins!

Discussion Cards

Directions: Use these cards with the *Family Discussions* game on page 32.

If you could be any superhero, who would you be and why?

If you could invent anything, what would it be and how would it help people?

If you could meet anyone, past or present, who would it be and what would you ask that person?

What do you believe is the most important job? Why?

If you could be any animal, what would it be and why?

If you could be really good at something, what would it be and why?

If you could only eat the same meal every day for the rest of your life, what would it be and why?

What is the most important thing in the world? Why?

Family Discussions

Family Discussions

Family Discussions

Family Discussions

Family Discussions

Family Discussions

Family Discussions

Family Discussions

Math Problems Flashcards

Directions: Use these cards with the *Who Can Solve It?* game on page 52.

$108 \div 9 =$	$144 \div 6 =$
$243 \div 9 =$	$115 \div 5 =$
$267 \div 3 =$	$21 \times 17 =$
$56 \times 10 =$	$45 \times 43 =$
$12 \times 16 =$	$82 \times 34 =$

Who Can Solve It?

Who Can Solve It?

Who Can Solve It?

Who Can Solve It?

Who Can Solve It?

Who Can Solve It?

Who Can Solve It?

Who Can Solve It?

Who Can Solve It?

Who Can Solve It?

Direction Cards

Directions: Use these cards with the *Toothpicks and Squares* game on page 62.

Take away four toothpicks to make only one square.

Take away two toothpicks to make three equal squares.

Take away one toothpick. Then, move four toothpicks to make 10 squares.

Take away two toothpicks to make two rectangles.

Move two toothpicks to make seven squares.

Toothpicks and Squares

Toothpicks and Squares

Toothpicks and Squares

Toothpicks and Squares

Toothpicks and Squares

Word Cards

Directions: Use these cards with the *Word Sentences* game on page 92.

coco	dogs
face	gash
hoax	loot
maze	nail
oink	pear
read	saws

Word Sentences

Word Sentences

Word Sentences

Word Sentences

Word Sentences

Word Sentences

Word Sentences

Word Sentences

Word Sentences

Word Sentences

Word Sentences

Word Sentences

Category Cards

Directions: Use these cards with the *Categories* game on page 102.

Categories

1. girl's name

2. sports team

3. science term

4. historical figure

5. item found at school

Categories

1. girl's name

2. sports team

3. science term

4. historical figure

5. item found at school

Categories

1. girl's name

2. sports team

3. science term

4. historical figure

5. item found at school

Categories

1. girl's name

2. sports team

3. science term

4. historical figure

5. item found at school

Categories

Categories

Categories

Categories

Letter Cards

Directions: Use these cards with the *Categories* game on page 102.

a	b	c
d	e	f
g	h	i
j	k	l
m	n	o
p	q	r
s	t	u
v	w	x
y	z	

Categories | Categories | Categories

Categories | Categories | Categories

Categories | Categories | Categories

Categories | Categories | Categories

Categories | Categories | Categories

Categories | Categories | Categories

Categories | Categories | Categories

Categories | Categories | Categories

Categorios | Catogorios

Answer Key

Week 1

It's All Relative! (page 14)

1. that
2. who
3. whose
4. which
5. whom
6. which

A Visit with Penguins (page 15)

1. Check that sentence(s) include some of the main ideas of the passage.
2. Check that response includes a prediction and a reason to support it.

Circus Balloon (page 16)

Check that written response includes descriptive words and details.

T-Shirt Designer (page 17)

Check that the T-shirt design is for a charity.

Raffle Tickets (page 18)

1. 6,942; six thousand, nine hundred forty-two
2. 10,753; ten thousand, seven hundred fifty-three
3. 24,197; twenty-four thousand, one hundred ninety-seven
4. 40,735; forty thousand, seven hundred thirty-five
5. 61,217; sixty-one thousand, two hundred seventeen
6. 81,369; eighty-one thousand, three hundred sixty-nine
7. 6,194; six thousand, one hundred ninety-four
8. 16,591; sixteen thousand, five hundred ninety-one
9. 84,894; eighty-four thousand, eight hundred ninety-four

Calculating Area (page 19)

1. 15 ft.^{2}
2. 2,322 cm^2
3. 1,250 m^2
4. 108 ft.^{2}

Solving by Estimating (page 20)

1. 10 cats
2. 30 boxes
3. 1,700 points

Which Explorer Went Where? (page 21)

Francisco Pizarro—Conquered the Incas

Ferdinand Magellan—The first to travel around the world

Christopher Columbus—Sailed with the *Niña, Pinta,* and *Santa Maria*

Hernán Cortés—Caused the fall of the Aztec empire

Roll-the-Numbers Multiplication Game (page 22)

Check that multiplication is done correctly.

Week 2

Sentence Emergencies (page 24)

1. **The** students in **Mr. Garcia's** class were reading **Charlotte's Web.**
2. **What** a wonderful day it is**!**
3. **Jordan,** come play with us in **Griffith Park.**
4. **Watch** out, **Michelle!**

Reading a Shake Recipe (page 25)

1. C
2. D

Read All About It! (page 26)

Check that newspaper article contains the *who, what, when, where, why,* and *how.*

Hollywood Star (page 27)

Check that the flyer describes the movie with pictures and words.

Answer Key (cont.)

Express This Number (page 28)

1. thirty-four thousand, two hundred sixty-two; 30,000 + 4,000 + 200 + 60 + 2

2. seven hundred eighty-one thousand, four hundred fifteen; 700,000 + 80,000 + 1,000 + 400 + 10 + 5

3. 51,527; 50,000 + 1,000 + 500 + 20 + 7

4. 923,334; 900,000 + 20,000 + 3,000 + 300 + 30 + 4

5. 23,469; twenty-three thousand, four hundred sixty-nine

Line Them Up: Making Line Plots (page 29)

1.

		x		x			
	x	x	x	x	x		x
x	x	x	x	x	x	x	x
1 in.	$1\frac{1}{4}$ in.	$1\frac{3}{4}$ in.	2 in.	$2\frac{1}{2}$ in.	$2\frac{3}{4}$ in.	$3\frac{1}{4}$ in.	$3\frac{1}{2}$ in.

2. $1\frac{3}{4}$ inches and $2\frac{1}{2}$ inches

3. $3\frac{1}{2}$ inches

4. 1 inch

5. $2\frac{1}{2}$ inches

Multistep Word Problems (page 30)

1. 47 stamps

2. 11 strawberries

3. Yes; $0.25

Many Ways to Say 10 (page 31)

20 ÷ 2	8 + 2	10 x 1	20 x .5	100 ÷ 10	15 − 5
15 − 5	20 x .5	100 ÷ 10	8 + 2	10 x 1	20 ÷ 2
100 ÷ 10	15 − 5	20 x .5	20 ÷ 2	8 + 2	10 x 1
8 + 2	10 x 1	20 ÷ 2	100 ÷ 10	15 − 5	20 x .5
20 x .5	100 ÷ 10	15 − 5	10 x 1	20 ÷ 2	8 + 2
10 x 1	20 ÷ 2	8 + 2	15 − 5	20 x .5	100 ÷ 10

Family Discussions (page 32)

Check that responses are not repeated and each person discusses the similarities and differences between responses.

Week 3

Stop That Sentence! (page 34)

1. My books are on the table. My math book is on top.

2. They were closing the store. It was time to go home.

3. Watch out for the slippery ice. You could fall and hurt yourself.

4. I got a new blue shirt. My blue shoes match perfectly.

5. My brother made the team. Will I be able to play baseball someday?

It's a Matter of Opinion (page 35)

The opinion sentence is *Everybody needs to have a pet.* Answer may include: The author supports the opinion with reasons and evidence about the benefits of pets that will convince the reader to believe that everyone needs one.

You're a Star! (page 36)

Check that the story explains how and why he or she became famous and other important things he or she might do in the future.

The Most Outrageous Dog Park (page 37)

Check that the symbols on the legend are clearly marked on the diagram.

Let's Compare! (page 38)

1. 65,812 < 79,458

2. 512,327 > 87,959

3. 672,735 < 673,736

4. 783,583 = 783,583

5. 23,428 < 32,482

6. 521,708 > 512,945

7. 834,499 = 834,499

8. 107,368 < 392,010

Answer Key (cont.)

Making Equivalent Fractions (page 39)

The following are some example answers:

1. $\frac{2}{3} = \frac{6}{9} = \frac{18}{27}$
2. $\frac{3}{8} = \frac{6}{16} = \frac{12}{32}$
3. $\frac{4}{5} = \frac{16}{20} = \frac{64}{80}$
4. $\frac{9}{10} = \frac{27}{30} = \frac{81}{90}$
5. $\frac{8}{13} = \frac{16}{26} = \frac{32}{52}$

Fraction Word Problems (page 40)

1. They ate $\frac{3}{4}$ of a pizza.
2. He made $\frac{4}{10}$ or $\frac{2}{5}$ of his shots.
3. She used 15 eggs.

Dinner Table Seating Chart (page 41)

George Washington	Benjamin Franklin	James Madison
Thomas Jefferson	John Adams	Alexander Hamilton

There may be other solutions. Check that the placement of the names represent the clues.

The Tallest Paper Tower (page 42)

Check that each player answers the discussion questions.

Week 4

To, Too, or Two? (page 44)

1. I'm going **to** be in a dance recital tomorrow. I'll be wearing my new tutu, which is a little **too** big. **Two** of my friends will dance, **too**. I'm **too** excited **to** sleep, but I have **to** go **to** bed.

2. The leaves were falling from the trees as I walked **to** school. It must be fall, which I call autumn, **too**. I know that there are **two** more weeks until Halloween. I can't wait **to** go trick-or-treating! My friend Alexa is going **to** walk with me, **too**. We will remember **to** say "Thank you!" after we get our candy. I hope that I get at least **two** lollipops **to** eat!

An Author's Use of Evidence (page 45)

The following are example answers:

1. The author uses such evidence as "Over an hour passed before we were seated, and no one apologized for this inconvenience" and "The server was quite rude when we asked for the items that we ordered."

2. The restaurant manager will likely change his actions since the customer made it clear that he wants to be a loyal customer but would like to see improvements. The restaurant manager will assume other customers feel this way, and the restaurant may lose business if it continues in this fashion.

Letter to the Mayor (page 46)

Check that response includes a proper opening and closing for a letter.

Room Designer Extraordinaire! (page 47)

Check that the room includes pictures for each category.

Rounding Decimals (page 48)

1. 51
2. 96
3. 21
4. 5.9
5. 13.7
6. 45.3
7. 3.91
8. 851.43
9. 0.63
10. Answer may include: *Because there is no denomination for $0.001, and $0.01 is the smallest denomination, so you must round to the nearest hundredth when dealing with money.*

Match the Fraction (page 49)

1. C
2. D
3. F
4. A
5. E
6. B

Answer Key *(cont.)*

Real World Fractions (page 50)

1. $12 \times \frac{3}{4} = \frac{36}{4} = 9$ pencils
2. $24 \times \frac{1}{3} = \frac{24}{3} = 8$ cupcakes
3. $18 \times \frac{2}{3} = \frac{36}{3} = 12$; $18 - 12 = 6$ balls

Connect the Dots (page 51)

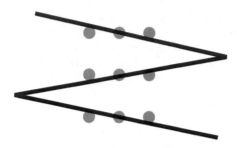

Check that responses describe how the puzzle was solved and how many tries were attempted.

Who Can Solve It? (page 52)

$108 \div 9 = 12$	$21 \times 17 = 357$
$144 \div 6 = 24$	$56 \times 10 = 560$
$243 \div 9 = 27$	$45 \times 43 = 1935$
$115 \div 5 = 23$	$12 \times 16 = 192$
$267 \div 3 = 89$	$82 \times 34 = 2788$

Week 5

Adjectives and Adverbs (page 54)

The following are example answers:

1. The small dog barked rapidly at the large, lazy cat.
2. I somehow hit the speeding ball hastily.
3. Mei Ling ravenously ate lunch.
4. Everyone enthusiastically watched Rafael energetically play basketball.

Inferring from a Picture (page 55)

The following are example answers:

1. The animals might be introducing or getting to know each other. The animals look curious.
2. They are facing each other so that they can check each other out.

It's Alive! (page 56)

Check that the response includes facts and details about the chosen domain and that information was found from credible sources.

True Identity (page 57)

Check that the face has features added to reveal a person's identity.

Multiply Using a Standard Algorithm (page 58)

1. row 1: 92; row 2: 1,380; row 3: 1,472
2. row 1: 459; row 2: 3,060; row 3: 3,519
3. row 1: 100; row 2: 2,000; row 3: 2,100
4. row 1: 564; row 2: 940; row 3: 1,504
5. 192 notebooks and 288 folders

Turning a Fraction into a Decimal (page 59)

1. 0.5
2. 0.9
3. 0.2
4. 0.07
5. 0.04
6. 0.26
7. 0.08
8. 0.4
9. 0.06
10. 0.98

Answer Key *(cont.)*

Features of Shapes (page 60)

1. right triangle

2. rectangle

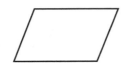

3. trapezoid

4. parallelogram

5. acute triangle

6. square

Awesome Analogies (page 61)

1. pig : oink :: dog : bark

2. duck : quack :: cow : moo

3. fish : swim :: cheetah : run

4. today : tomorrow :: yesterday : today

5. gray : black :: pink : red

Check that analogies are written correctly.

Toothpicks and Squares (page 62)

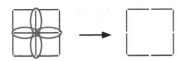

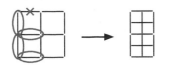

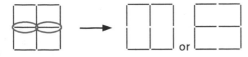

Week 6

Put Them in Order (page 64)

The sequence of the sentences should be as follows:

I woke up one morning . . . I got out of bed . . . What a shock I got when . . . I ran to my mother . . . She said, "It appears that those seeds . . ." Then she looked . . . I am feeling better now . . .

Identifying Text Structure (page 65)

Text structure: Chronology

Evidence: The text includes events or steps in order of how they happen. The text contains such signal words as *First*, *Next*, and *Then*.

Movie Review (page 66)

Check that review includes details about the plot, descriptions of the characters, and details to support the main idea.

There's a Hole in My Paper (page 67)

Check that the picture includes the hole.

What's Remaining? (page 68)

1. 1 R1

2. 4 R3

3. 16

4. 21 R3

5. 14 R4

6. 7 R1

7. 108

8. 14 R1

9. 25

Answer Key (cont.)

Getting Decimals in Line (page 69)

1. 0.9, 0.5, 0.07, 0.06
2. 0.9, 0.061, 0.06, 0.04
3. 0.8, 0.4, 0.12, 0.002
4. 0.9, 0.57, 0.09, 0.006

5.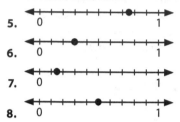
6.
7.
8.

Fraction Party Riddles (page 70)

1. 10 pounds of ribs
2. $7\frac{1}{5}$ pounds of salmon
3. 4 pies

What Happened? (page 71)

Jack is a fish, and his tank has broken. He landed in the boot on the floor next to the table. Water and glass from the tank surround the boot on the floor.

Your child is the driver, so the eye color of the driver is whatever color he or she has.

Move Those Things! (page 72)

Check that players do not touch the items with their hands and that each utensil is used one time.

Week 7

Clue Me In! (page 74)

Clue: never found on its own

Definition: removed by pulling or cutting out

Clue: just about everywhere

Definition: large amount of something

A Letter of Despair (page 75)

Multiple parts may be underlined. Some examples include: *I have never imagined such horror as I have seen these last few days at Shiloh; The first day of fighting was a clear Southern victory; I lived through the bloodiest day of the war thus far; General Johnston himself was slain by a cannon blast, and General Beauregard took over command; Our own dear friends, Kurt Flanders and Willem Simpson, fell; My heart grieves for them and for their families back home in Georgia; General Buell arrived with Grant's reinforcements; In the end, General Beauregard was forced to withdraw our troops back to Corinth. Comments in the margin should reflect the child's feelings.*

That's Funny! (page 76)

Check that response is about a funny or embarrassing moment.

What's Does It Look Like? (page 77)

Check that the steps are detailed.

Get the Message! (page 78)

T	37 R12	U	284	D	92 R1
A	150	J	152 R18	N	304 R5
G	237 R3	B	1,242 R4	O	19
W	73 R3	E	25	Y	22 R2
V	15 R3	H	33 R6	R	8 R3

Message: Whatever you are, be a good one.

Accurate Areas (page 79)

1. 15 cm²
2. 12 cm²
3. 16 cm²
4. 30 cm²
5. 180 cm²
6. 30 cm²
7. 16 cm²
8. 36 cm²

Answer Key *(cont.)*

How Long Does It Take? (page 80)

1. A. 7 hours, 20 minutes; B. 3 hours, 50 minutes;
   C. 4 hours, 35 minutes; D. 1 hour, 5 minutes;
   E. 5 hours, 45 minutes; F. 4 hours, 15 minutes
2. 2 hours, 15 minutes
3. 12:52 P.M.
4. 10:20 A.M.
5. A. 375 minutes; B. 6 hours, 15 minutes

Who Is Responsible for What? (page 81)

1. Susan B. Anthony
2. Lewis and Clark
3. Martin Luther King Jr.
4. James Madison
5. Benjamin Franklin
6. Teddy Roosevelt

Dough Boats (page 82)

Make sure that the winning boat stays afloat. Be sure to answer the discussion questions.

Week 8

Idioms (page 84)

The following are example answers:

1. She meant that the movie was amazing.
2. He meant that his father would not stand for it any longer.
3. She meant that she would be leaving.
4. He meant that he was not feeling well.
5. He meant that he slept very deeply.

The Crazier the Better (page 85)

1. José likes Crazy Hair Day because he "loved being goofy, and he loved making his classmates laugh." Crazy Hair Day lets José do both of those things.
2. In third grade, José "braided his hair into 16 tiny braids." Then, he "wrapped a pipe cleaner around each braid and stuck paper airplanes to the ends" and called the design Fly Boy.
3. José is planning to use the bird's nest for Crazy Hair Day. "It was going to be the perfect Crazy Hair Day accessory!"

Here's How You Do It! (page 86)

Check that response is in correct step-by-step order.

The Most Amazing Machine (page 87)

Check that the picture and notes describe the machine.

Looking for a Pattern Problems (page 88)

Problem A

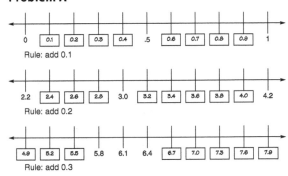

Rule: add 0.1

Rule: add 0.2

Rule: add 0.3

Problem B

Check that the number line and rule match.

Target Number (page 89)

The following are example answers:

1. $1 + 2 = 3$; $(4 - 3) \times 3 = 3$; $(4 + 2) \div 2 = 3$
2. $8 - 6 = 2$; $10 - 8 = 2$ $(7 + 9) \div 8 = 2$; $(7 + 9) - (6 + 8) = 2$
3. $3 + 3 + 6 = 12$; $5 \times 3 - 3 = 12$; $(6 \times 3) - (3 + 3) = 12$
4. $(5 \times 10) \div 10 = 5$; $(4 \times 10) \div (4 + 4) = 5$; $10 - 5 = 5$

Consumer Math (page 90)

1. $10.38
2. No, she will be under by $1.95.
3. $13.83
4. 36 cups

Answer Key (cont.)

How Does He Have Blue Eyes? (page 91)

The mother has blue eyes, meaning her genotype is bb. For their son to have blue eyes, the brown-eyed father must carry a genotype of Bb.

Word Sentences (page 92)

Check that each letter in the words on the cards is used in the sentence.

Week 9

Order of Adjectives (page 94)

The following are example answers:

1. My dad is funny, thin, and tan.
2. Pizza is delicious, round, and cheesy.
3. Dogs are intelligent, furry, and companionable.
4. Football is exciting, intense, and entertaining.

What Is the Theme? (page 95)

The following are example answers:

1. The theme of the poem is that anything is possible when you use your imagination.
2. The author uses lines such as "But I can be happy building at home. / Let the sofa be mountains, the carpet be sea" to let readers know the theme is imagination.

My Family from Different View Points (page 96)

Check that both responses are written from another person's point of view.

Thumbprint Pictures (page 97)

Check that the pictures are drawn around the thumbprints.

Solve That Notation: Unknown Quantities (page 98)

1. 4×10^4
2. 7.5×10^4
3. 3×10^3
4. 1×10^5
5. 8.3×10^1
6. 9.56×10^2
7. 6,000
8. 80,000
9. 300
10. 29,000
11. 9,100
12. 150

Triangles (page 99)

1. isosceles; right
2. equilateral; acute
3. isosceles; acute

Solve That Word Problem! (page 100)

1. 38 cars
2. 0 jumping jacks
3. Yes; 3 slices are left.

What Doesn't Belong? (page 101)

1. Brazil does not belong because it is in South America and the other places are all in North America.
2. Germany does not belong because it is not in Asia like the other places.
3. India does not belong because it is a country and not a continent.
4. The Andes Mountains does not belong because it is a mountain range and the other places are bodies of water.
5. Mexico does not belong because it is a country and the other things listed are all cities in the world.

Categories (page 102)

Check that players use the correct letter for each category.

Parent Handbook

Dear Parents or Guardians,

Have you ever wondered why states have learning standards? Teachers used to determine what they would cover based on what content was included in their textbooks. That seems crazy! Why would educators put publishers in charge of determining what they should teach? Luckily, we've moved past that time period into one where educational professionals create standards. These standards direct teachers on what students should know and be able to do at each grade level. As a parent, it's your job to make sure you understand the standards! That way, you can help your child be ready for school.

The following pages are a quick guide to help you better understand both the standards and how they are being taught. There are also suggestions for ways you can help as you work with your child at home.

Here's to successful kids!

Sincerely,

The Shell Education Staff

College and Career Readiness Standards

Today's college and career readiness standards, including the Common Core State Standards and other national standards, have created more consistency among states in how they teach math and English language arts. In the past, state departments of education had their own standards for each grade level. The problem was, what was taught at a specific grade in one state may have been taught at a different grade in another state. This made it difficult when students moved from state to state.

Today, many states have adopted new standards. This means that for the first time, there is better consistency in what is being taught at each grade level across the states, with the ultimate goal of getting students ready to be successful in college and in their careers.

Standards Features

The overall goal for the standards is to better prepare students for life. Today's standards use several key features:

- They describe what students should know and be able to do at each grade level.

- They are rigorous.

- They require higher-level thinking.

- They are aimed at making sure students are prepared for college and/or their future careers.

- They require students to explain and justify answers.

Mathematical Standards

There are several ways that today's mathematics standards have shifted to improve upon previous standards. The following are some of the shifts that have been made.

Focus

Instead of covering a lot of topics lightly, today's standards focus on a few key areas at much deeper levels. Only focusing on a few concepts each year allows students more time to understand the grade-level concepts.

How Can You Help?	What Can You Say?
Provide paper or manipulatives (such as beans or pieces of cereal) as your child is working so that he or she can show his or her answer.	Is there another way you can show the answer?
Have your child explain his or her thinking or the way he or she got the answer.	What did you do to solve the problem? What were you thinking as you solved the problem?

Coherence

The standards covered for each grade are more closely connected to each other. In addition, each grade's standards are more closely connected to the previous grade and the following grade.

How Can You Help?	What Can You Say?
Help your child to make connections to other concepts he or she has learned.	What else have you learned that could help you understand this concept?
Ask your child to circle words that may help him or her make connections to previously learned concepts.	What words in the directions (or in the word problem) help you know how to solve the problem?

Fluency

The standards drive students to perform mathematical computations with speed and accuracy. This is done through memorization and repetition. Students need to know the most efficient way to solve problems, too!

How Can You Help?	What Can You Say?
Help your child identify patterns that will work for increasing speed and accuracy.	What numbers do you know that can help you solve this problem?
Encourage the most efficient way to solve problems.	Can you get the same answer in a different way? Is there an easier way to solve the problem?

Mathematical Standards *(cont.)*

Deep Understanding

Students must develop a very good understanding of mathematical concepts. A deep understanding of mathematical concepts ensures that students know the *how* and the *why* behind what they are doing.

How Can You Help?	What Can You Say?
Encourage your child to make a model of the answer.	How do you know your answer is correct? Can you show your answer in a different way?
Have your child explain the steps he or she uses to solve problems.	Can you teach me to solve the problem?

Application

Today's standards call for more rigor. Students need to have strong conceptual understandings, be able to use math fluently, and apply the right math skills in different situations.

How Can You Help?	What Can You Say?
Encourage your child to use multiple methods for solving and showing his or her answers.	Can you explain your answer in a different way?
Have your child circle words or numbers that provide information on how to solve the problem.	What words gave you clues about how to solve this problem?

Dual Intensity

Students need to develop good understandings of mathematical concepts and then practice those concepts.

How Can You Help?	What Can You Say?
Provide practice on concepts or basic facts your child is having trouble with.	What did you have difficulty with? How can you practice that?
Have your child identify where his or her breakdown in understanding is when solving a problem.	Where can you find the help you need?

Language Arts Standards

The following charts describe the key shifts in language arts standards and some great ways that you can help your child achieve with them.

Balancing Informational and Literary Texts

Students should read and have books read aloud to them that represent a variety of texts and have a balance of informational and literary texts.

How Can You Help?	What Can You Say?
Find topics your child is interested in and then find both fiction and nonfiction books on the topic.	Since you like dinosaurs, let's find a story about dinosaurs and an informational book that tells facts about dinosaurs!
Encourage your child to know features of informational and literary texts.	How do you know this book is informational? What features does this literary book have?

Knowledge in the Disciplines

Once students reach sixth grade, they are expected to gain information directly through content-area texts rather than have the information told to them. Younger students can read nonfiction texts to prepare for this transition in the middle grades.

How Can You Help?	What Can You Say?
Talk about science and social studies topics with your child in everyday conversations so that your child learns about related words and concepts.	I heard on the news that there will be a lunar eclipse tonight. Let's watch it together so that we can see the shadow of Earth come between the moon and the sun.
Provide a variety of experiences for your child so that he or she can use them when reading about a topic. It makes the topic easier to understand.	Let's go have fun exploring the tide pools! What do you think we will see there? (*ask before*) What did you see at the tide pools? (*ask after*)

Staircase of Complexity

Students should read grade-appropriate complex texts. They may not understand the content right away, but with support and time, they will eventually comprehend what they're reading.

How Can You Help?	What Can You Say?
Know your child's reading level. Help your child find books that are at the high end of your child's reading level.	I found these three books for you to read. Which one interests you?
Read books to your child that are above his or her reading level. It exposes him or her to more complex vocabulary, sentences, and ideas.	Which book would you like me to read to you?

Language Arts Standards (cont.)

Text-Based Answers

Students should be able to answer questions and defend their positions using evidence from texts. This evidence can include illustrations and other graphics.

How Can You Help?	What Can You Say?
Ask your child to explain his or her answer using evidence from a book.	How do you know that? How else do you know _____?
Ask your child to look for evidence about something you notice in a book.	What evidence is there that _____?

Writing from Sources

Students should easily reference the texts they are reading as they write about them.

How Can You Help?	What Can You Say?
Have your child underline in the text the answers to questions he or she is answering through writing.	Where is the evidence in the text? How can you include that in your written response?
Provide sentence frames to help your child reference the text.	On page _____, the author says _____.

Academic Vocabulary

Academic vocabulary is a student's ability to recognize, understand, and use more sophisticated words in both reading and writing. Having a strong vocabulary allows students to access more complex texts.

How Can You Help?	What Can You Say?
Model using precise vocabulary.	I noticed you used the word _____. Could you have used a stronger word?
Provide a wide variety of experiences for your child to learn new words. These experiences don't have to cost money. They can be simple, everyday activities!	We are going to get the oil changed in the car. I want you to see if you can find the mechanic in his overalls.